New Edition

ST. LUCIA

Travel Guide 2024

BY JAMES ATLAS VENTURE

ST. LUCIA

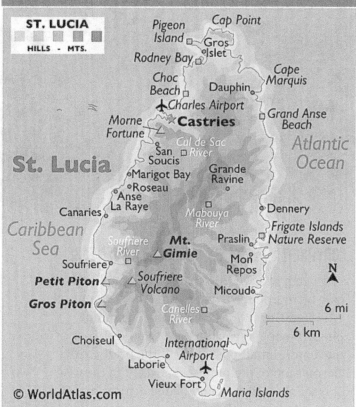

ST. LUCIA
HILLS - MTS.

Pigeon Island
Cap Point
Gros Islet
Rodney Bay
Choc Beach
Dauphin
Cape Marquis
Charles Airport
Morne Fortune
Castries
Grand Anse Beach
San Soucis
Cul de Sac River
Atlantic Ocean
St. Lucia
Marigot Bay
Roseau
Anse La Raye
Grande Ravine
Canaries
Mabouya River
Dennery
Caribbean Sea
Soufriere River
Mt. △**Gimie**
Praslin
Frigate Islands Nature Reserve
Soufriere
Mon Repos
N
Petit Piton
Soufriere Volcano
Micoud
Gros Piton
Canelles River
6 mi
6 km
Choiseul
International Airport
Laborie
Vieux Fort
Maria Islands

© WorldAtlas.com

1. Open the camera app on your phone or tablet.
2. Point the camera at the QR code, making sure it's centered and in focus.
3. Hold the camera steady for a few seconds to allow the code to be detected.
4. Tap the pop-up notification or prompt to open the link or perform the action associated with the QR code.
5. Wait for the action to complete, such as opening a website, downloading an app, or displaying a message.

3

TABLE OF CONTENTS

CHAPTER 1: INTRODUCTION TO SAINT LUCIA

 elcome to Saint Lucia, a tropical paradise nestled in the heart of the Caribbean. Known for its lush landscapes, vibrant culture, and warm hospitality, Saint Lucia is the perfect destination for travelers seeking both adventure and relaxation. This introduction will provide you with everything you need to know before embarking on your journey to this enchanting island.

Saint Lucia is located in the eastern Caribbean Sea, bordered by the Atlantic Ocean to the east. It is part of the Lesser Antilles and lies north of Saint Vincent and the Grenadines, northwest of Barbados, and south of Martinique. The island spans just 27 miles in length and 14 miles in width, yet it offers a diverse range of landscapes, from pristine beaches and turquoise waters to lush rainforests and the towering Piton mountains, a UNESCO World Heritage Site.

The culture of Saint Lucia is a rich tapestry woven from African, French, and British influences. The island's history as a colonial battleground between the French and British has left a unique cultural legacy, evident in the island's language, cuisine, and traditions. English is the official language, but you'll also hear Saint Lucian Creole, a French-based patois, spoken by locals. The island's music scene is lively, with calypso, reggae, and soca beats providing the soundtrack to local festivals and daily life. The Saint Lucia Jazz and Arts Festival, held annually, is a highlight that draws international visitors and showcases the island's artistic talents.

Saint Lucia's history is as captivating as its scenery. The island was originally inhabited by the Arawak and Carib peoples before European colonization began in the 17th century. The French and British vied for control of the island, which changed hands 14 times before the British finally secured it in 1814.

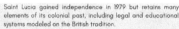

Saint Lucia gained independence in 1979 but retains many elements of its colonial past, including legal and educational systems modeled on the British tradition.

When it comes to attractions, Saint Lucia is a treasure trove of natural wonders and historic sites. The iconic Pitons, Gros Piton, and Petit Piton, are twin volcanic spires that rise majestically from the sea and offer breathtaking hiking opportunities. The Sulphur Springs, located near the town of Soufrière, is the world's only drive in volcano and a popular spot for mud baths and hot springs. Pigeon Island National Park, a former British military base, now serves as a scenic site for hiking, picnicking, and exploring historical ruins. The island's beaches, such as Reduit Beach and Anse Chastanet, are perfect for sunbathing, snorkeling, and diving in the clear Caribbean waters.

Saint Lucia's currency is the Eastern Caribbean dollar (XCD), but US dollars are widely accepted in most tourist areas. The island operates on a parliamentary democracy system, and visitors should be aware of local laws and customs.

As you prepare for your trip to Saint Lucia, know that you are about to experience a destination that is as welcoming as it is beautiful. From its stunning natural landscapes to its rich cultural heritage, Saint Lucia offers a unique and unforgettable travel experience. So pack your bags, bring your sense of adventure, and get ready to discover all that this Caribbean gem has to offer.

Brief History and Cultural Overview

Saint Lucia's history is as captivating as its natural beauty, offering a rich tapestry woven from centuries of diverse influences. The island was first inhabited by the peaceful Arawak people around 200 AD, who named it "Iouanalao," meaning "Land of the Iguanas." By the 9th century, the more warlike Caribs had displaced the Arawaks, renaming the island "Hewanorra."

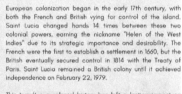

European colonization began in the early 17th century, with both the French and British vying for control of the island. Saint Lucia changed hands 14 times between these two colonial powers, earning the nickname "Helen of the West Indies" due to its strategic importance and desirability. The French were the first to establish a settlement in 1660, but the British eventually secured control in 1814 with the Treaty of Paris. Saint Lucia remained a British colony until it achieved independence on February 22, 1979.

This tumultuous colonial history has left a lasting impact on Saint Lucia's culture, creating a vibrant blend of African, French, and British influences. English is the official language, reflecting the island's British heritage, but Saint Lucian Creole, a French-based patois, is widely spoken and adds a unique flavor to local communication.

The island's music and dance traditions, including calypso, reggae, and the uniquely Saint Lucian soca, are integral parts of its cultural identity and are celebrated during festivals such as the annual Saint Lucia Carnival and the renowned Saint Lucia Jazz and Arts Festival.

Saint Lucia's culinary landscape is equally diverse, combining African, French, and Caribbean flavors to create mouthwatering dishes like bouyon (a hearty meat and vegetable stew), green fig and saltfish (the national dish), and callaloo soup. The island's markets are vibrant with the colors and scents of fresh produce, spices, and local crafts, offering a sensory experience that reflects the island's rich cultural heritage.

Religion plays a significant role in daily life, with Roman Catholicism being the predominant faith due to the French colonial influence. However, various Protestant denominations and other religions are also practiced, reflecting the island's diverse population.

Saint Lucians are known for their warmth, hospitality, and a strong sense of community, making visitors feel welcome and at home. This cultural richness, coupled with the island's stunning natural beauty, makes Saint Lucia a truly unique and unforgettable destination.

Key Highlights and Attractions

Saint Lucia is a treasure trove of natural wonders and cultural gems, offering visitors a plethora of attractions that highlight the island's beauty and heritage. From its iconic volcanic peaks to its lush rainforests and pristine beaches, Saint Lucia promises an unforgettable experience for every traveler.

The island's most famous landmarks are the Pitons, two majestic volcanic spires rising dramatically from the sea. Gros Piton and Petit Piton, designated a UNESCO World Heritage Site, are a must-visit for their breathtaking views and challenging hikes. Whether you're an avid climber or simply enjoy stunning scenery, the Pitons provide a spectacular backdrop for any adventure.

Another unique attraction is the Sulphur Springs, located near Soufrière. Known as the world's only drive-in volcano, this geothermal wonder allows you to drive right up to the bubbling mud pools and steaming vents. Visitors can indulge in a therapeutic mud bath, believed to have healing properties, and then rinse off in the nearby warm sulfur springs, leaving their skin rejuvenated. For history buffs, Pigeon Island National Park offers a fascinating glimpse into Saint Lucia's past. Once a strategic military outpost used by the British, the park is now a serene spot for hiking, picnicking, and exploring historical ruins. Climb to the top of Fort Rodney for panoramic views of the island and the Caribbean Sea.

Saint Lucia's beaches are another highlight, each offering its own unique charm. Reduit Beach, with its golden sands and calm waters, is perfect for families and water sports enthusiasts. For a more secluded experience, visit Anse Chastanet, where the black sand beach is framed by lush greenery and coral reefs teeming with marine life, ideal for snorkeling and diving.

Nature lovers will be captivated by the island's rainforests, where you can embark on zip-lining adventures, guided hikes, and bird-watching tours. The Enbas Saut Waterfall Trail and the Tet Paul Nature Trail offer stunning vistas and the chance to spot exotic wildlife.

Saint Lucia's vibrant culture is best experienced through its festivals and local markets. The annual Saint Lucia Carnival is a colorful explosion of music, dance, and costumes, while the Saint Lucia Jazz and Arts Festival attracts international artists and showcases the island's artistic talent.

Whether you're exploring the Pitons, relaxing on a beach, or immersing yourself in the local culture, Saint Lucia offers a diverse array of attractions that cater to all interests, ensuring an unforgettable Caribbean adventure.

CHAPTER 2: PLANNING YOUR TRIP

P lanning your trip to Saint Lucia is an exciting part of the adventure. Start by choosing the best time to visit, typically from December to April for the dry season. Book your flights and accommodations early to secure the best deals, considering options from luxury resorts to charming Airbnb rentals. Ensure your travel documents are up to date, including a valid passport. Research transportation options for getting around the island, whether by rental car, taxi, or local buses. Pack essentials like light clothing, sunscreen, and travel adapters, and don't forget travel insurance for a worry-free vacation.

BEST TIME TO VISIT

Choosing the perfect time to visit Saint Lucia can greatly enhance your travel experience, as the island's climate and events vary throughout the year. Saint Lucia enjoys a tropical climate, which means warm temperatures year-round, but understanding the seasonal differences will help you make the most of your trip.

The best time to visit Saint Lucia is generally from December to April, during the island's dry season. This period offers the most consistent weather, with plenty of sunshine and minimal rainfall, making it ideal for beach activities, outdoor adventures, and exploring the island's natural beauty.

Temperatures typically range from the mid-70s to the mid-80s Fahrenheit (24-29°C), providing perfect conditions for sunbathing, snorkeling, hiking, and attending local festivals.

The dry season also coincides with the peak tourist season, so expect vibrant atmospheres, bustling markets, and lively events like the Saint Lucia Jazz and Arts Festival in May.

While the dry season is popular, visiting during the shoulder months of May and November can also be a great option. These months offer a balance of good weather and fewer crowds. Hotel rates and flight prices are often lower, providing better value for travelers. You can still enjoy plenty of sunshine with occasional rain showers, which help keep the island lush and green.

From June to November, Saint Lucia experiences its wet season, with increased rainfall and the possibility of hurricanes. While this might deter some travelers, there are still benefits to visiting during this time. The island is less crowded, allowing for a more relaxed and intimate experience. Rain showers are usually brief and can be refreshing, especially in the heat. Plus, the island's flora is at its most vibrant, and waterfalls are more impressive. If you decide to visit during the wet season, it's wise to keep an eye on weather forecasts and consider travel insurance.

Ultimately, the best time to visit Saint Lucia depends on your preferences. If you enjoy lively festivals and guaranteed sunshine, the dry season is perfect. If you prefer a quieter, more budget-friendly trip with a lush, green landscape, consider the shoulder months or even the wet season. Regardless of when you visit, Saint Lucia's natural beauty, warm hospitality, and diverse attractions will ensure an unforgettable experience.

Visa and Entry Requirements

Planning a trip to Saint Lucia involves understanding the visa and entry requirements to ensure a smooth and hassle-free arrival. Fortunately, Saint Lucia's entry process is straightforward for most travelers, making it an accessible and welcoming destination.

Citizens of many countries, including the United States, Canada, the United Kingdom, and the European Union, do not require a visa for short stays, typically up to 42 days. Upon arrival, you will need a valid passport with at least six months remaining before expiration and a return or onward ticket. It's always a good idea to check the latest entry requirements from your country of origin before traveling, as regulations can change.

For travelers from countries that do require a visa, the process is relatively simple. You can apply for a tourist visa at a Saint Lucian embassy or consulate in your home country. The required documents usually include a completed visa application form, a valid passport, passport-sized photos, proof of accommodation, and a return or onward ticket. The processing time for a visa can vary, so it's wise to apply well in advance of your planned travel dates.

Upon arrival in Saint Lucia, you will go through standard immigration procedures. Be prepared to present your passport, completed immigration form, and proof of accommodation. The immigration officers are friendly and efficient, ensuring your entry is as smooth as possible.

In addition to your passport and visa (if required), it's important to have all necessary travel documents in order. This includes your travel itinerary, hotel reservations, and any travel insurance documents. Having these readily available can help expedite your entry process and ensure you're fully prepared for your stay.

Saint Lucia also has specific health requirements, especially in light of global health concerns. It's recommended to check any vaccination requirements or health advisories before you travel. This information can typically be found on the official Saint Lucian tourism or government websites.

Visiting Saint Lucia is relatively straightforward for most travelers. Ensuring you have a valid passport, necessary visas, and relevant travel documents will make your arrival smooth and stress-free. With your entry requirements in order, you can focus on enjoying the island's breathtaking beauty and warm hospitality from the moment you arrive.

Travel Documents

Preparing the necessary travel documents is a crucial step to ensure a smooth and enjoyable trip to Saint Lucia. Whether you're planning a relaxing beach vacation, an adventurous hike up the Pitons, or an exploration of the island's rich cultural heritage, having your paperwork in order will help you start your journey worry-free.

First and foremost, you need a valid passport. Your passport should be valid for at least six months beyond your planned departure date from Saint Lucia. This is a common requirement for international travel and helps avoid any issues with entry or re-entry into your home country.

For many travelers, including those from the United States, Canada, the United Kingdom, and the European Union, a visa is not required for short stays, typically up to 42 days. However, always double-check the latest entry requirements based on your nationality, as policies can change. If you do need a visa, apply well in advance at a Saint Lucian embassy or consulate, ensuring you have all required documents, such as a completed visa application form, passport-sized photos, proof of accommodation, and a return or onward ticket.

In addition to your passport and visa (if applicable), you'll need a return or onward ticket. This proof of onward travel is often checked by airlines before you board your flight to Saint Lucia and by immigration officials upon arrival. It demonstrates that you have plans to leave the island and helps streamline your entry process.

It's also advisable to carry proof of accommodation, such as hotel reservations or a confirmation from an Airbnb host. This can be helpful at immigration checkpoints and provides peace of mind knowing that your lodging arrangements are confirmed.

Travel insurance is another essential document. While not always mandatory, having comprehensive travel insurance can protect you against unexpected medical expenses, trip cancellations, or lost luggage. Make sure your insurance covers the duration of your stay and any activities you plan to undertake.

Lastly, keep copies of important documents like your passport, visa, travel insurance, and accommodation confirmations. Store these copies separately from the originals, either in a different bag or digitally, so you have backups in case anything gets lost or stolen.

By organizing these travel documents ahead of time, you'll be well-prepared for your trip to Saint Lucia, allowing you to focus on soaking up the sun, exploring the island's beauty, and enjoying its vibrant culture.

Travel Insurance Recommendations

Travel insurance is an essential part of planning a trip to Saint Lucia, offering peace of mind and protection against unexpected events. Whether you're exploring the island's lush rainforests, relaxing on its pristine beaches, or enjoying local festivals, having the right insurance can ensure your journey remains enjoyable and worry-free.

When choosing travel insurance, consider the coverage options that best suit your needs. Medical coverage is crucial, as it protects you against the high costs of medical treatment abroad. Look for a policy that includes emergency medical expenses, hospitalization, and medical evacuation. Even though Saint Lucia has good healthcare facilities, being covered for emergencies ensures you receive the best care without the financial burden.

Trip cancellation and interruption coverage is another important aspect. This coverage reimburses you for non-refundable trip costs if you have to cancel or cut short your trip due to unforeseen circumstances like illness, severe weather, or family emergencies. Given the unpredictability of travel plans, this feature can save you a significant amount of money.

Lost, stolen, or damaged baggage coverage is also beneficial. It provides compensation for your belongings if your luggage is lost, delayed, or damaged during your trip. Considering the inconvenience of losing essential items while on vacation, this coverage helps you replace necessities quickly.

For adventure enthusiasts, make sure your travel insurance covers activities you plan to engage in. Saint Lucia offers a range of exciting adventures, from hiking the Pitons to snorkeling in vibrant coral reefs. Ensure your policy includes coverage for these activities, as some insurers may exclude high-risk sports or require additional premiums.

When comparing policies, pay attention to the policy limits, deductibles, and exclusions. A higher policy limit means better coverage but might come with a higher premium. Deductibles are the amount you pay out of pocket before the insurance kicks in, so choose a balance that suits your budget and coverage needs.

It's also wise to check the insurer's reputation and customer service. Reading reviews and ratings can give you an idea of their reliability and how they handle claims. Opt for a well-established insurance provider with a good track record of customer satisfaction.

Comprehensive travel insurance is a must for any trip to Saint Lucia. By selecting a policy with adequate medical coverage, trip cancellation protection, baggage coverage, and adventure activity inclusion, you can travel with confidence, knowing you're protected against the unexpected. This allows you to focus on enjoying the island's natural beauty and rich culture, ensuring a memorable and stress-free vacation.

Travel kits and Essentials

Comfortable walking shoes or sandals are essential for exploring the island's natural trails and attractions. A reusable water bottle will help you stay hydrated, and a small daypack can carry your essentials while you're out and about.

Lastly, bring copies of important documents like your passport, travel insurance, and accommodation confirmations. Having both digital and physical copies ensures you're prepared in case of emergencies.

With these travel kits and essentials, you'll be ready to fully enjoy the beauty and adventures that Saint Lucia has to offer.

Start with lightweight, breathable clothing suitable for the tropical climate. Pack swimwear, sun hats, and sunglasses to protect yourself from the sun, and bring a light rain jacket for unexpected showers.

Don't forget your toiletries, including sunscreen with high SPF, insect repellent, and any personal hygiene items. A basic first aid kit with band-aids, antiseptic wipes, and any prescription medications is also a must.

For your electronics, pack a universal power adapter and chargers for your devices. A waterproof phone case can be handy for beach days or snorkeling trips. Consider bringing a portable charger to keep your devices powered during day-long excursions.

Electronics and Gadgets

If you enjoy reading or relaxing with music, consider bringing a lightweight e-reader or a portable Bluetooth speaker. These gadgets can provide entertainment during downtime or while lounging on the beach.

For underwater enthusiasts, a waterproof case for your smartphone or a waterproof camera is ideal for capturing underwater adventures while snorkeling or diving in Saint Lucia's crystal-clear waters.

By packing these electronics and gadgets, you'll be well-equipped to capture memories, stay connected, and make the most of your unforgettable trip to Saint Lucia.

Safety Instruments

Ensuring your safety while exploring Saint Lucia involves packing a few essential safety instruments. Start with a reliable travel lock to secure your luggage and hotel room, providing peace of mind when you're out exploring the island. A money belt or hidden wallet can also help safeguard your valuables while you're on the move.

When venturing into nature or participating in water activities, consider packing a compact first aid kit with basic supplies like band-aids, antiseptic wipes, and pain relievers. This kit can come in handy for minor injuries or unexpected incidents during your adventures.

For sun protection, pack high SPF sunscreen, a wide-brimmed hat, and sunglasses to shield yourself from the strong Caribbean sun. Insect repellent is also essential, particularly if you plan on exploring forested areas or hiking trails.

If you're planning adventurous activities such as hiking the Pitons or exploring volcanic sites, a sturdy pair of hiking shoes with good grip is recommended. Ensure your footwear is comfortable and suitable for various terrains to prevent slips or falls.

By packing these safety instruments, you'll be well-prepared to enjoy all that Saint Lucia has to offer while prioritizing your comfort and well-being throughout your journey.

CHAPTER 3: GETTING THERE AND AROUND

S t. Lucia is accessible by international flights landing at Hewanorra International Airport in the south and George F. L. Charles Airport in the north. Once on the island, rental cars, taxis, and local minibusses are available for getting around. The island's winding roads offer scenic drives, while water taxis provide a unique perspective on coastal travel.

FLIGHTS AND AIRPORTS

Arriving in Saint Lucia is a seamless experience with two main airports serving the island: Hewanorra International Airport (UVF) in Vieux Fort and George F. L. Charles Airport (SLU) near Castries. Hewanorra International Airport is the larger and more frequently used airport, handling international flights from major cities worldwide. It's located approximately an hour's drive from the popular tourist areas in the south of the island.

George F. L. Charles Airport primarily serves inter-Caribbean flights and regional connections. It's conveniently located just outside Castries, the capital city, making it a convenient choice for travelers heading directly to the northern part of the island.

Both airports offer modern facilities, including duty-free shopping, restaurants, car rental services, and transportation options to nearby hotels and resorts. Immigration and customs procedures are generally efficient and straightforward, ensuring a smooth entry into Saint Lucia.

Upon arrival, taxis and rental cars are readily available for transportation to your accommodation. Many resorts also offer shuttle services for guests, making it easy to start your vacation without delay.

Whether you're arriving for a relaxing beach getaway, an adventurous eco-tour, or a romantic retreat, Saint Lucia's airports provide a welcoming gateway to your Caribbean adventure.

Transportation Options (Car Rentals, Taxis, Buses)

From the freedom of driving yourself to the convenience of taxis and the local charm of public buses, each option offers unique advantages for navigating this Caribbean gem.

Car Rentals: Renting a car in Saint Lucia provides unparalleled freedom to explore the island at your own pace. Both Hewanorra International Airport and George F. L. Charles Airport host reputable car rental agencies offering a range of vehicles from compact cars to SUVs. Driving follows British rules, with vehicles on the left-hand side. While roads can be narrow and winding, especially in rural areas, cautious driving ensures a safe and scenic journey.

Taxis: Taxis are a readily available and comfortable mode of transport, ideal for travelers seeking hassle-free transfers between airports, hotels, and attractions. Fares are usually negotiated upfront or metered, so it's wise to confirm the price before starting your trip. Taxis provide flexibility for short excursions or when driving yourself isn't preferred.

Public Buses: For an authentic local experience, Saint Lucia's public buses offer an economical way to travel. Operating on fixed routes across the island, buses serve both residents and tourists, connecting major destinations like Castries, Soufrière, and Gros Islet. While buses may be crowded during peak times, they provide an insight into everyday life on the island and are a budget-friendly option for exploring beyond tourist hubs.

Navigating transportation in Saint Lucia allows you to tailor your journey to fit your itinerary and preferences. Whether you prioritize independence with a rental car, seek convenience with taxis, or embrace local culture on public buses, each option enhances your experience, ensuring a memorable and flexible exploration of Saint Lucia's natural beauty and vibrant culture.

Tips for Getting Around the Island

Navigating Saint Lucia efficiently enhances your experience, allowing you to discover its stunning landscapes and cultural treasures with ease. Here are some helpful tips for getting around the island:

Plan Your Routes: Before setting out, familiarize yourself with the island's geography and major attractions. This helps optimize your itinerary and minimizes travel time between destinations.

Renting a Car: Consider renting a car for flexibility and independence. Ensure your rental includes a GPS or a reliable map to navigate unfamiliar roads. Remember to drive on the left-hand side, following British driving rules.

Taxi Services: Taxis are widely available and convenient for short trips or airport transfers. Negotiate fares upfront or ensure the meter is used to avoid surprises. Taxis provide door-to-door service, making them a stress-free option for exploring specific locations.

Public Buses: Embrace local culture by taking public buses, which offer affordable fares and connect major towns and attractions. Be prepared for varying schedules and potential crowdedness during peak times.

Walking and Hiking: Many attractions in Saint Lucia are best explored on foot, such as exploring local markets or hiking trails. Wear comfortable shoes, especially for visits to natural reserves like the Tet Paul Nature Trail or Gros Piton.

Boat Tours and Ferries: To explore coastal attractions or nearby islands like Martinique, consider booking boat tours or using inter-island ferry services. These provide unique perspectives of Saint Lucia's coastline and neighboring regions.

Cycling: For active travelers, cycling offers a scenic way to explore coastal roads and rural landscapes. Rent bikes from local shops or join guided cycling tours for a memorable adventure.

Local Insights: Don't hesitate to ask locals for recommendations on transportation and hidden gems. They often provide valuable tips on navigating the island efficiently and discovering lesser-known spots.

By combining these tips with your itinerary, you'll navigate Saint Lucia smoothly, allowing you to focus on enjoying its natural beauty, rich history, and warm hospitality throughout your journey.

CHAPTER 4: ACCOMMODATION OPTIONS

S t. Lucia offers a wide range of accommodations, from luxurious all-inclusive resorts and boutique hotels to charming guesthouses and vacation rentals. Whether you seek a beachfront escape, a secluded retreat in the rainforest, or a budget-friendly stay, the island caters to various preferences and budgets, ensuring a comfortable experience for all visitors.

TOP HOTELS: ROMANTIC, LUXURY, AND BUDGET-FRIENDLY OPTIONS

Saint Lucia offers a diverse array of accommodations to suit every traveler's needs, from romantic retreats to luxurious resorts and budget-friendly options. Each category promises a unique experience, ensuring a memorable stay on this beautiful Caribbean island.

Romantic Hotels: Anse Chastanet, located in Soufrière, Saint Lucia, offers stunning views, unique architecture, and two beautiful beaches. Enjoy activities like snorkeling, scuba diving, and jungle biking. Experience fresh, organic dining and luxurious spa treatments. For reservations, contact Anse Chastanet at +1 855-647-7578.

Anse Chastanet

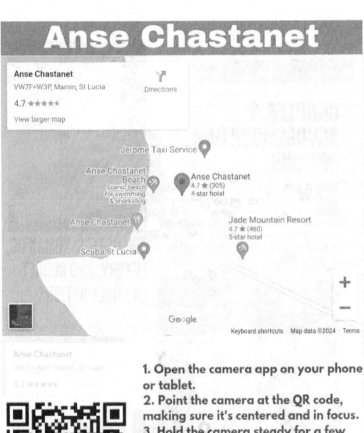

Anse Chastanet
VW7F+W3P, Marnin, St Lucia

Directions

4.7 ★★★★★

View larger map

Jerome Taxi Service

Anse Chastanet
Beach
Scenic beach
for swimming
& snorkeling

Anse Chastanet
4.7 ★ (305)
4-star hotel

Anse Chastanet

Jade Mountain Resort
4.7 ★ (460)
5-star hotel

Scuba St Lucia

Google

Keyboard shortcuts   Map data ©2024   Terms

1. Open the camera app on your phone or tablet.
2. Point the camera at the QR code, making sure it's centered and in focus.
3. Hold the camera steady for a few seconds to allow the code to be detected.
4. Tap the pop-up notification or prompt to open the link or perform the action associated with the QR code.
5. Wait for the action to complete, such as opening a website, downloading an app, or displaying a message.

28

For couples seeking a romantic getaway, Saint Lucia is home to several enchanting hotels that provide intimate settings and stunning views. Jade Mountain is a top choice, renowned for its breathtaking architecture and mesmerizing views of the Pitons. Each suite, known as a "sanctuary," features an open fourth wall, allowing uninterrupted vistas of the mountains and the Caribbean Sea, along with private infinity pools.

Jade Mountain

Jade Mountain Resort

VW7F+GG3, Mamin, St Lucia

Directions

4.7 ★★★★★

View larger map

for swimming
& snorkeling
4-star hotel

Anse Chastanet

Jade Mountain Club
Caribbean

Scuba St Lucia

Jade Mountain Resort
4.7 ★ (460)
5-star hotel

Google

Keyboard shortcuts | Map data ©2024 | Terms

1. Open the camera app on your phone or tablet.
2. Point the camera at the QR code, making sure it's centered and in focus.
3. Hold the camera steady for a few seconds to allow the code to be detected.
4. Tap the pop-up notification or prompt to open the link or perform the action associated with the QR code.
5. Wait for the action to complete, such as opening a website, downloading an app, or displaying a message.

Another favorite is Ladera Resort, perched on a ridge overlooking the Pitons and the sea.

This adults-only resort offers luxurious suites with open-air designs, private plunge pools, and romantic touches like in-room massages and candlelit dinners. Sugar Beach, A Viceroy Resort, nestled in a lush rainforest, offers elegant villas and beachfront bungalows perfect for couples looking to escape into a serene paradise.

Luxury Hotels: Saint Lucia's luxury hotels cater to discerning travelers seeking top-notch amenities and unparalleled service. The Landings Resort and Spa offers spacious, opulent suites with private terraces and plunge pools, as well as a world-class spa and fine dining restaurants. The resort's private marina provides easy access to water activities like sailing and snorkeling.

Cap Maison, a boutique hotel on the northern tip of the island, boasts exquisite villa-style accommodations, an award-winning restaurant, and a secluded beach. The resort's cliff-top location offers stunning panoramic views, making it an ideal spot for indulgence and relaxation.

For those who prefer a larger resort, Sandals Grande St. Lucian delivers with all-inclusive luxury, offering multiple dining options, water sports, and beautiful beachfront settings. The over-the-water bungalows are particularly popular, providing an exclusive and immersive experience.

Budget-Friendly Hotels: Travelers on a budget will find plenty of welcoming and affordable options in Saint Lucia. Bay Gardens Hotel in Rodney Bay offers comfortable accommodations with easy access to the beach, shops, and local attractions. Guests can enjoy amenities like free Wi-Fi, a swimming pool, and complimentary shuttle service to the nearby Bay Gardens Beach Resort.

Coco Palm is another excellent choice, combining affordability with charm and convenience. Located in the heart of Rodney Bay Village, it features a pool, restaurant, and tropical garden setting. Rooms are tastefully decorated, offering comfort and value for money.

For a more intimate experience, Harmony Suites provides spacious, well-appointed suites in a tranquil setting near Rodney Bay Marina. This small, family-owned hotel emphasizes personalized service and affordability, making it a popular choice among budget-conscious travelers.

Whether you're looking for a romantic escape, a luxurious retreat, or a budget-friendly stay, Saint Lucia's diverse hotel offerings ensure that every visitor can find the perfect accommodation to suit their needs and preferences. Each hotel category provides unique experiences, allowing you to immerse yourself fully in the island's natural beauty and vibrant culture.

Airbnb Options

St. Lucia offers a variety of Airbnb options that cater to different preferences and budgets, making it an excellent choice for travelers. Whether you are looking for a cozy cottage in the heart of Soufriere or a luxurious villa with panoramic views of Marigot Bay, you'll find something to suit your needs.

For those seeking a central location, the Cozy Cottage in Soufriere offers modern amenities and proximity to local attractions like the Sulphur Springs and Hummingbird Beach. If you're looking for something more spacious, Villa Annona at Nature's Paradise provides stunning views and is surrounded by a botanical garden.

Many properties are equipped with essential amenities such as Wi-Fi, air conditioning, and fully equipped kitchens, ensuring a comfortable stay. Additionally, beach house rentals in areas like Gros Islet and Laborie offer private pools and easy access to the beach, perfect for a relaxing getaway.

No matter your preference, St. Lucia's Airbnb listings provide diverse options to enhance your travel experience.

Unique Stays (Eco-lodges, Boutique Hotels)

When it comes to unique stays in St. Lucia, the island offers a delightful array of eco-lodges and boutique hotels that provide an immersive experience blending luxury with sustainability. These accommodations not only showcase the natural beauty of St. Lucia but also emphasize environmental responsibility and local culture.

One notable option is the Balenbouche Estate, an eco-friendly retreat that offers a serene escape amidst lush landscapes and historical charm. This family-run estate focuses on sustainable practices and provides visitors with an authentic St. Lucian experience through its rustic cottages and organic farm.

For those seeking a luxurious yet eco-conscious stay, the Fond Doux Plantation & Resort is a perfect choice. This boutique hotel, nestled in a 19th-century working plantation, combines historical architecture with modern amenities. Guests can stay in charming cottages surrounded by tropical gardens and enjoy organic cuisine sourced from the plantation itself.

Another exceptional stay is the Calabash Mountain Villa, which offers stunning views of the surrounding mountains and forests. This eco-lodge is designed to harmonize with the natural environment, featuring solar energy and rainwater harvesting systems. These unique stays not only offer comfort and luxury but also ensure that your visit to St. Lucia is both environmentally friendly and culturally enriching. Whether you're drawn to the historical charm of Balenbouche Estate, the plantation experience at Fond Doux, or the scenic beauty of Calabash Mountain Villa, St. Lucia's eco-lodges and boutique hotels promise an unforgettable and sustainable vacation.

CHAPTER 5: WEATHER AND LOCATION IN S.T LUCIA

S t. Lucia boasts a tropical climate with warm, consistent temperatures year-round, typically averaging around 27°C (80°F). The island experiences two primary seasons: the dry season and the rainy season. The dry season, from December to May,is characterized by minimal rainfall and plenty of sunshine, making it an ideal time for outdoor activities and beach vacations.

Conversely, the rainy season, spanning June to November, brings higher humidity and frequent rain showers, which can sometimes be heavy but usually short-lived. During this period, the island is also at a higher risk for tropical storms and hurricanes, particularly in the peak months of August and September.

Despite the rain, the lush, green landscapes of St. Lucia thrive during this time, offering a vibrant and picturesque setting. The island's climate and weather patterns are conducive to a variety of outdoor adventures, from hiking the famous Pitons to exploring the diverse marine life in the surrounding waters. Whether visiting during the dry or rainy season, St. Lucia's tropical weather ensures a warm and welcoming environment for travelers year-round.

Saint Lucia is a beautiful Caribbean island known for its diverse geography and stunning landscapes. Covering an area of 238 square miles (616 square kilometers), the island is situated between Saint Vincent to the south and Martinique to the north. Saint Lucia's landscape is predominantly volcanic and mountainous, featuring fertile valleys and lush forests. The island's highest peak is Mount Gimie, rising to 950 meters, while the iconic twin Pitons—Gros Piton and Petit Piton—are striking natural landmarks located south of Soufriere.

The island's coastline stretches for 98 miles (158 kilometers), offering sandy beaches and numerous coves perfect for water activities. The capital city, Castries, is located in the northwest, set on a natural harbor that has been central to the island's development. Other key settlements include fishing villages and banana farming areas scattered around the island.

Rainfall in Saint Lucia is plentiful but varies by region, with the mountainous interior receiving the most precipitation. The island experiences a wet-dry seasonal cycle, though this is not very pronounced. The natural resources of Saint Lucia include forests, mineral springs, and geothermal potential, contributing to its rich biodiversity and making it a haven for eco-tourism.

The island's strategic geographic coordinates are 13°53′N latitude and 60°58′W longitude, placing it within the UTC-4 time zone, one hour ahead of Washington, D.C., during standard time.

CHAPTER 6: CURRENCY AND COMMUNICATION

S aint Lucia uses the East Caribbean Dollar (XCD), which is shared with several other countries in the region, including Antigua and Barbuda, Dominica, Grenada, and Saint Kitts and Nevis. The East Caribbean Dollar is abbreviated as EC$. The exchange rate between the East Caribbean Dollar and the US Dollar is fixed, with 1 USD equaling approximately 2.70 XCD.

This fixed rate makes it relatively straightforward for travelers from the United States to manage their finances while in Saint Lucia. For those carrying other currencies, it is advisable to exchange money at local banks or authorized exchange services to get the best rates.

While credit and debit cards are accepted at many hotels, restaurants, and larger establishments, cash is still king for smaller vendors, markets, and local services. It's recommended to carry some EC$ for convenience. ATMs are available across the island, providing easy access to local currency. For the latest and most accurate exchange rates, you can refer to resources such as the Eastern Caribbean Central Bank or reputable financial services websites.

Currency Exchange Tips

When exchanging currency for your trip to Saint Lucia, there are several key tips to keep in mind to ensure you get the best rates and manage your money efficiently. First, it's a good idea to exchange some money before you leave for Saint Lucia. This can help you avoid less favorable rates and higher fees at airports or hotels upon arrival. Once in Saint Lucia, aim to use local banks or authorized exchange services for the best rates, as they are generally more favorable compared to airports or hotels.

ATMs are widely available across the island and can be a convenient way to withdraw local currency, the Eastern Caribbean Dollar (EC$). However, be aware of any foreign transaction fees your bank may charge. Additionally, major credit and debit cards are accepted in most hotels, restaurants, and larger stores, and using cards can often give you a better exchange rate compared to cash exchanges. It's essential to check with your card provider about any foreign transaction fees.

When exchanging money, try to obtain small denominations. These are useful for tipping, paying for small purchases, and using local transportation. Monitoring exchange rates before and during your trip using reliable financial websites or apps can help you determine the best times and places to exchange your money. Be cautious of dynamic currency conversion, where merchants offer to charge your card in your home currency rather than the local currency. This often results in less favorable rates and additional fees, so it's best to pay in the local currency.

Safety is also important when carrying cash. Avoid displaying large amounts of money and use hotel safes to store excess cash and valuables. Keeping receipts of your currency exchanges and ATM withdrawals can help you track your spending and resolve any disputes that may arise.

By following these tips, you can efficiently manage your currency exchange and make the most of your financial resources during your stay in Saint Lucia.

Language Overview

Saint Lucia is a multilingual island, with English as its official language. English is widely used in government, business, and education, making it the primary medium of communication. However, the island's cultural diversity is reflected in its linguistic landscape.

A significant portion of the population speaks Saint Lucian Creole French, also known as Kwéyòl or Patwa. This Creole language is derived from French and incorporates elements of African languages, Carib, and other influences. Kwéyòl is an important part of the island's cultural heritage and is spoken in everyday conversation, especially in informal settings. It is also used in music, storytelling, and other cultural expressions.

The use of Kwéyòl is promoted through various cultural initiatives, including Jounen Kwéyòl (Creole Day), celebrated annually to honor and preserve the Creole language and culture. This event features traditional music, dance, food, and dress, showcasing the island's rich Creole heritage.

In addition to English and Kwéyòl, Spanish and French are also taught in schools due to the island's proximity to other Caribbean and Latin American nations and the historical influence of French colonization. This multilingual environment enhances Saint Lucia's cultural richness and facilitates communication with visitors from diverse backgrounds.

Overall, the linguistic diversity of Saint Lucia reflects its complex history and vibrant culture, making it a unique destination for travelers interested in experiencing the island's rich heritage.

50 Basic Communication Words for Tourists

50 Basic Communication Words for Tourists

1. Hello - Bonjou
2. Goodbye - Orevwa
3. Please - Souple
4. Thank you - Mèsi
5. Yes - Wi
6. No - Non

7. Excuse me - Eskize mwen
8. Sorry - Pardon
9. Help - Èd
10. Where - Kote
11. When - Kilè
12. How much - Konbyen
13. What - Sa
14. Who - Ki moun
15. Why - Poukisa
16. Which - Ki
17. Can you - Eske ou kapab
18. Do you have - Èske ou genyen
19. I need - Mwen bezwen
20. I want - Mwen vle
21. Water - Dlo
22. Food - Manje
23. Bathroom - Twalet
24. Hotel - Otel
25. Taxi - Taksi
26. Bus - Bis
27. Airport - Ayewopò
28. Bank - Labank
29. Police - Lapolis
30. Hospital - Lopital
31. Doctor - Doktè
32. Pharmacy - Famasi
33. Shop - Boutik
34. Restaurant - Restoran
35. Beach - Plaj
36. Market - Mache
37. Museum - Mize

38. Tour - Vwayaj
39. Ticket - Tikè
40. Left - Gòch
41. Right - Dwat
42. Straight - Dwat devan
43. Here - Isi
44. There - Laba
45. Open - Louvri
46. Closed - Fèmen
47. Entrance - Antre
48. Exit - Sòti

These words and phrases will help you navigate and communicate more easily during your travels in St. Lucia.

Mobile Network and Internet Access

St. Lucia offers reliable mobile network and internet access, making it easy for tourists to stay connected during their visit. The island is served by two primary mobile service providers, Digicel and Flow, both of which offer extensive coverage across the island. Whether you're in the bustling capital of Castries, the picturesque town of Soufrière, or exploring remote beaches, you'll generally find good mobile reception.

For visitors, obtaining a local SIM card is straightforward. Both Digicel and Flow have outlets at the Hewanorra International Airport and in major towns, where you can purchase a SIM card and choose from various prepaid plans. These plans often include generous data allowances, making it easy to access maps, stay in touch with loved ones, or share your travel experiences on social media.

In addition to mobile networks, St. Lucia provides ample internet access. Most hotels, resorts, and guesthouses offer complimentary Wi-Fi to their guests. Public Wi-Fi is also available in some cafes, restaurants, and public areas, particularly in popular tourist spots. However, the speed and reliability of public Wi-Fi can vary, so it's advisable to use a mobile data plan for more consistent internet access.

For those who need to stay connected for work or other important matters, portable Wi-Fi devices are available for rent. These devices offer high-speed internet access and can connect multiple devices simultaneously, providing a convenient solution for families or groups traveling together.

Overall, staying connected in St. Lucia is relatively hassle-free. With reliable mobile networks and widespread internet access, you can navigate the island with ease, stay in touch with friends and family, and make the most of your Caribbean adventure.

Useful Mobile Apps

Google Maps: Google Maps is indispensable for navigating the island. It offers detailed maps, driving directions, and information about local businesses, attractions, and restaurants. The app also provides real-time traffic updates, making it easier to plan your routes.

TripAdvisor: TripAdvisor is great for discovering top-rated attractions, restaurants, and accommodations in St. Lucia. You can read reviews from other travelers, compare prices, and even book tours and activities directly through the app.

XE Currency: XE Currency is an essential app for managing your finances while traveling. It provides real-time currency exchange rates and allows you to convert prices into your home currency, helping you stay on top of your budget.

Duolingo: Duolingo is a fun and interactive language-learning app. Although English is widely spoken in St. Lucia, picking up a few phrases in French Creole can enhance your cultural experience and help you connect with locals.

WhatsApp: WhatsApp is a popular messaging app that allows you to stay in touch with friends and family back home without incurring international SMS charges. It supports text, voice, and video calls, making it a versatile communication tool.

Google Translate: Google Translate can help you understand and communicate in different languages. It's particularly useful for translating signs, menus, and other written materials, as well as for real-time conversation translation.

My Digicel or My Flow: If you purchase a local SIM card from Digicel or Flow, their respective apps—My Digicel or My Flow—are useful for managing your mobile plan. You can check your data balance, top up your account, and purchase additional services through these apps.

Uber or Lyft: While St. Lucia doesn't have Uber or Lyft services, local taxi apps like Karib Cable or local ride-sharing services can be very useful for booking rides, especially in more populated areas.

WeatherBug: WeatherBug provides real-time weather updates, forecasts, and alerts, helping you plan your daily activities around the tropical climate of St. Lucia.

PackPoint: PackPoint is a smart packing list app that helps you organize what to bring based on the length of your stay, the weather at your destination, and any activities you have planned.

By downloading these apps, you can make your trip to St. Lucia more convenient, enjoyable, and stress-free.

CHAPTER 7: SAFETY AND HEALTH

W hen traveling to St. Lucia, maintaining your health and hygiene is essential to ensure a safe and enjoyable trip.

Stay Hydrated: The tropical climate in St. Lucia can be hot and humid. Make sure to drink plenty of water throughout the day to stay hydrated. Carry a reusable water bottle with you and refill it regularly.

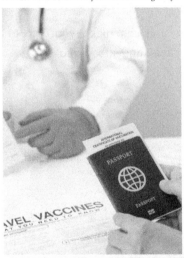

Protect Yourself from the Sun: The sun in St. Lucia can be intense, so protect your skin by applying a broad-spectrum sunscreen with a high SPF. Wear a hat, sunglasses, and lightweight, long-sleeved clothing to shield yourself from the sun's rays. Reapply sunscreen every two hours, especially after swimming or sweating.

Prevent Mosquito Bites: Mosquitoes in tropical regions can carry diseases such as dengue fever and Zika virus. Use insect repellent containing DEET or other effective ingredients, and wear long-sleeved shirts and long pants, especially during dawn and dusk when mosquitoes are most active. Consider sleeping under a mosquito net if you're staying in an area where mosquito-borne illnesses are a concern.

Practice Good Hand Hygiene: Wash your hands regularly with soap and water, especially before eating or touching your face. If soap and water are not available, use a hand sanitizer with at least 60% alcohol. This helps prevent the spread of germs and reduces the risk of illness.

Eat and Drink Safely: Stick to well-cooked food and avoid raw or undercooked dishes. Be cautious with street food and make sure it's prepared in a clean environment. Drink bottled or filtered water, and avoid ice cubes made from tap water. Opt for fruits that you can peel yourself, such as bananas and oranges.

Stay Active Safely: Engage in physical activities like hiking, swimming, or exploring the island, but do so safely. Wear appropriate footwear, use safety gear when needed, and be aware of your surroundings. If you plan to engage in water sports, ensure the equipment is in good condition and follow safety guidelines.

Know Where to Get Medical Help: Familiarize yourself with the location of the nearest medical facilities and pharmacies. Carry a basic first aid kit with essentials like band-aids, antiseptic wipes, pain relievers, and any prescription medications you need. In case of an emergency, having this information readily available can be crucial.

Practice Safe Swimming: When swimming in the ocean, be mindful of currents and tides. Swim in designated areas, follow lifeguard instructions, and avoid swimming alone. If you're unsure about the safety of a particular beach or swimming area, ask locals or hotel staff for advice.

Manage Stress and Rest Well: Traveling can sometimes be stressful, so take time to relax and unwind. Get enough sleep each night to keep your immune system strong. Practice stress-relief techniques such as deep breathing, meditation, or yoga to maintain your mental well-being.

Be Prepared for Allergies and Sensitivities: If you have allergies or sensitivities, inform your hosts or hotel staff about your needs. Carry any necessary medications, such as antihistamines or epinephrine auto-injectors, and wear a medical alert bracelet if needed.

By following these health and hygiene tips, you can help ensure a safe, healthy, and enjoyable visit to St. Lucia.

Safety Tips and Local Laws

Stay Aware of Your Surroundings: While St. Lucia is generally safe, it's essential to stay vigilant, especially in crowded areas and tourist hotspots. Keep an eye on your belongings, and avoid displaying valuable items openly.

Use Reliable Transportation: When traveling around the island, use reputable transportation services. Licensed taxis and rental cars from well-known companies are recommended. Avoid accepting rides from strangers.

Be Cautious at Night: Exercise caution when going out at night. Stick to well-lit and populated areas. Avoid walking alone in secluded places after dark, and always inform someone of your whereabouts.

Secure Your Accommodations: Ensure your hotel or rental property has adequate security measures. Lock doors and windows when you leave your room. Use the hotel safe to store valuables and important documents.

Follow Beach and Water Safety Guidelines: Pay attention to safety flags and warnings on beaches. Swim in designated areas, and be mindful of strong currents. If you're not a strong swimmer, consider wearing a life jacket.

Practice Safe Driving: If you're renting a car, drive on the left side of the road, as St. Lucia follows the British driving system. Be cautious of narrow and winding roads. Use seat belts at all times, and avoid drinking and driving.

Respect Local Customs and Etiquette: St. Lucians are known for their friendly and hospitable nature. Show respect for local customs and traditions. Dress modestly when visiting religious sites and local communities.

Local Laws:

Drug Laws: The possession and use of illegal drugs, including marijuana, are prohibited in St. Lucia. Offenders can face severe penalties, including fines and imprisonment. Be aware that drug laws are strictly enforced.

Alcohol Consumption: The legal drinking age in St. Lucia is 18. It is illegal to consume alcohol in public places outside of licensed premises. Drinking and driving is strictly prohibited, and offenders can face heavy fines and imprisonment.

Beach Etiquette: Many of St. Lucia's beaches are public, but some may be privately owned by resorts. Respect the rules and regulations of private beaches, and avoid trespassing. Littering is frowned upon, so dispose of waste properly.

Photography Restrictions: While photography is generally allowed in public places, avoid taking pictures of individuals without their consent, especially in rural areas and local communities. Some religious sites and private properties may have restrictions on photography.

Environmental Protection: St. Lucia places a strong emphasis on environmental conservation. Do not disturb or damage coral reefs, marine life, or natural habitats. Avoid collecting shells, corals, or other natural souvenirs from the beach.

Driving Laws: To drive in St. Lucia, you need a valid driver's license from your home country or an International Driving Permit. Observe speed limits and traffic signs. Use seat belts at all times, and do not use mobile phones while driving.

Respect Wildlife: St. Lucia is home to diverse wildlife. Avoid feeding or approaching wild animals, as it can be dangerous for both you and the animals. Follow the guidelines of local wildlife authorities and tour operators.

By following these safety tips and understanding the local laws, you can have a safe and enjoyable experience in St. Lucia. Respecting the rules and customs of the island will help ensure a positive and memorable visit.

Emergency Contacts and Resources

When traveling in St. Lucia, it's essential to have quick access to emergency contacts and resources to ensure your safety and well-being. Here's a comprehensive list of emergency contacts and resources to keep handy during your visit:

Emergency Services:
- Police:
 - Phone: 999 or 911

- The Royal St. Lucia Police Force handles law enforcement and public safety.

- Fire Department:
  - Phone: 911
  - For fire-related emergencies, dial 911 for immediate assistance.

- Ambulance and Medical Emergencies:
  - Phone: 911
  - For medical emergencies, contact the ambulance service to get immediate help and transport to the nearest hospital.

Medical Facilities:
- Victoria Hospital:
  - Location: Castries
  - Phone: +1 758-452-2421
  - Victoria Hospital is one of the main public hospitals on the island, offering a range of medical services.

- St. Jude Hospital:
  - Location: Vieux Fort
  - Phone: +1 758-454-6041
  - Another key public hospital providing comprehensive healthcare services.

- Tapion Hospital:
  - Location: Castries
  - Phone: +1 758-459-2000
  - Tapion Hospital is a private facility offering various medical and surgical services.

Pharmacies:
- Pharmacies are widely available in St. Lucia, with many located in major towns and near hospitals. They can provide over-the-counter medications and fill prescriptions.

Tourist Assistance:
- St. Lucia Tourist Board:
  - Phone: +1 758-452-4094
  - The Tourist Board can provide information and assistance for travelers. Visit their website for more resources.

- Embassies and Consulates:
  - For foreign nationals, it's useful to have the contact details of your country's embassy or consulate in St. Lucia. They can offer assistance in emergencies, such as lost passports or legal issues.

Utilities and Services:
- Electricity Services:
  - St. Lucia Electricity Services Limited (LUCELEC)
  - Phone: +1 758-452-2165
  - For power outages or electrical issues.

- Water Services:
  - Water and Sewerage Company Inc. (WASCO)
  - Phone: +1 758-452-5344
  - For water supply issues or emergencies.

Telecommunications:
- In case of communication needs or technical issues, major telecommunications providers such as Digicel and FLOW offer customer support services.

Transportation:
- Hewanorra International Airport (UVF):
  - Location: Vieux Fort
  - Phone: +1 758-454-6355
  - For flight information and airport services.

- George F. L. Charles Airport (SLU):
  - Location: Castries
  - Phone: +1 758-452-2596
  - For domestic flight information and services.

- Taxi Services:
  - Taxis are a reliable mode of transport, and it's advisable to use licensed taxi services. Confirm fares before starting your journey.

Having these contacts and resources at your fingertips can significantly enhance your safety and preparedness while enjoying your stay in St. Lucia.

Chapter 8: Top Attractions and Activities

The Pitons of Saint Lucia are an iconic duo of volcanic spires that stand majestically on the island's southwestern dominating the landscape and offering some of the most breathtaking views in the Caribbean. Recognized as a UNESCO World Heritage Site, the Pitons consist of Gros Piton and Petit Piton, connected by the Pitons

Management Area (PMA), which spans both marine and terrestrial environments.

The Pitons

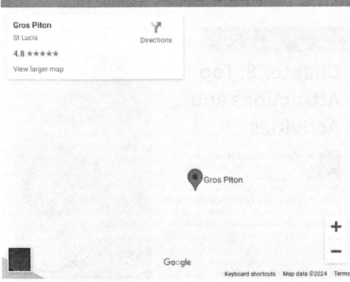

Gros Piton
St Lucia

4.8 ★★★★★

View larger map

Directions

Gros Piton

Google

Keyboard shortcuts   Map data ©2024   Terms

1. Open the camera app on your phone or tablet.
2. Point the camera at the QR code, making sure it's centered and in focus.
3. Hold the camera steady for a few seconds to allow the code to be detected.
4. Tap the pop-up notification or prompt to open the link or perform the action associated with the QR code.
5. Wait for the action to complete, such as opening a website, downloading an app, or displaying a message.

58

Gros Piton is the taller of the two, standing at approximately 2,530 feet. It is more accessible to hikers, even those without extensive mountaineering experience. The hike to the summit typically takes between two to four hours, depending on the hiker's pace and stamina. At the top, visitors are rewarded with panoramic views of the island and the Caribbean Sea. The climb, while challenging, is manageable with the guidance of local tour guides, who are trained to ensure safety and provide enriching information about the area.

Petit Piton, slightly shorter at 2,438 feet, presents a steeper and more demanding climb. While less frequented by casual hikers, it offers equally stunning vistas, including views of neighboring islands like St. Vincent, Barbados, Martinique, and Dominica. This peak is favored by more experienced climbers seeking a more intense hiking adventure.

The geological features of the Pitons are fascinating, including a geothermal field with hot springs known as Sulphur Springs, lava flows, and pyroclastic deposits. The diverse ecosystems in the PMA are home to a rich array of flora and fauna, including numerous rare species of plants and animals. The marine environment boasts vibrant coral reefs, making the area a paradise for snorkelers and divers.

Visiting the Pitons offers more than just a hike; it's an opportunity to immerse oneself in the natural beauty and geological wonders of Saint Lucia, providing a unique experience that combines adventure, education, and breathtaking natural scenery.

Sulphur Springs and Mud Baths

Sulphur Springs, located near the town of Soufrière in Saint Lucia, is often referred to as "the world's only drive-in volcano." This unique geological site offers visitors an unparalleled experience to witness volcanic activity up close, coupled with the therapeutic benefits of its famous mud baths.

Sulphur Springs was formed from a collapsed crater of the Qualibou volcano and is a bubbling cauldron of geothermal activity. Visitors can drive into the caldera, which is a rare feature for volcanic sites globally. The area is marked by steaming vents and boiling pools, releasing sulfurous gases that create a distinct, albeit pungent, aroma. This active geothermal field is a visual spectacle, with its colorful mineral deposits and continuous geothermal action.

Qualibou volcano

Qualibou
Malgretoute, St Lucia
4.5 ★★★★★
View larger map

Directions

Soufrière Drive In Volcano
Sulfur springs in a volcano caldera

Qualibou

Sulphur Springs Park Interpretation Centre

Google

Keyboard shortcuts   Map data ©2024   Terms

1. Open the camera app on your phone or tablet.
2. Point the camera at the QR code, making sure it's centered and in focus.
3. Hold the camera steady for a few seconds to allow the code to be detected.
4. Tap the pop-up notification or prompt to open the link or perform the action associated with the QR code.
5. Wait for the action to complete, such as opening a website, downloading an app, or displaying a message.

Mud Baths: One of the main attractions of Sulphur Springs is the naturally heated mud baths. These mud baths are rich in minerals such as sulfur, which are believed to have therapeutic properties. Bathers immerse themselves in the warm, thick mud, which is said to exfoliate the skin, relieve joint and muscle pain, and improve overall skin health. After the mud application, visitors rinse off in the nearby hot springs, leaving their skin feeling rejuvenated and smooth.

Health Benefits: The mud baths at Sulphur Springs are often touted for their health benefits. The high sulfur content is said to help with conditions like arthritis, eczema, and sore muscles. Additionally, the overall experience is incredibly relaxing, making it a popular activity for both tourists and locals seeking a natural spa experience.

Visiting Sulphur Springs: A visit to Sulphur Springs is a unique addition to any Saint Lucia itinerary. The site offers guided tours that provide insights into the geothermal activity and the history of the area. After the tour, visitors can indulge in the mud baths, making for a comprehensive and memorable experience. The site is well-equipped with facilities, including changing rooms and showers, to enhance the comfort and convenience of the visitors.

For more details or to plan a visit, you can contact Sulphur Springs at: 00 1 855-647-7578.

Sulphur Springs and its mud baths offer an extraordinary blend of adventure, relaxation, and natural wellness, making it a must-visit destination on the beautiful island of Saint Lucia.

Pigeon Island National Park

Pigeon Island National Park in Saint Lucia is a captivating destination brimming with history, natural beauty, and vibrant activities. Located just north of Castries, this 44-acre park was initially an island until a causeway connected it to the mainland in 1972. It holds significant historical value, having been a strategic military base during the colonial era, particularly under Admiral George Rodney during the late 18th century.

Visitors to Pigeon Island can explore the ruins of Fort Rodney, hike to scenic viewpoints offering panoramic views of the northwest coastline, and immerse themselves in the rich history at the Interpretation Centre. The park is home to two

beautiful beaches where you can relax or enjoy water activities, and there are restaurants on-site offering local cuisine and a historical pub.

Pigeon Island is not only a historical site but also a hub for cultural events. It hosts the Saint Lucia Jazz and Arts Festival each spring, drawing visitors for its vibrant concerts and artistic showcases. Additionally, the park is a popular venue for weddings, offering picturesque spots like gazebos and cliffside views for unforgettable ceremonies.

Access to Pigeon Island is convenient, whether by taxi, rental car, or public transportation, with numerous tours available that include transportation, refreshments, and guided experiences. Admission fees are reasonable, with the park open daily from 9 am to 5 pm.

1. Open the camera app on your phone or tablet.
2. Point the camera at the QR code, making sure it's centered and in focus.
3. Hold the camera steady for a few seconds to allow the code to be detected.
4. Tap the pop-up notification or prompt to open the link or perform the action associated with the QR code.
5. Wait for the action to complete, such as opening a website, downloading an app, or displaying a message.

Rainforest Adventures (Zip-lining, Hiking)

Saint Lucia's lush rainforests offer thrilling adventures for nature enthusiasts and thrill-seekers alike, with zip-lining and hiking experiences that showcase the island's stunning landscapes and biodiversity.

Zip-lining: Embark on an exhilarating zip-lining journey through the dense rainforest canopy, where adrenaline meets breathtaking views. Rainforest Adventures in Dennery offers one of the most popular zip-lining experiences on the island. Glide through the treetops on a series of zip lines, enjoying panoramic vistas of verdant valleys and glimpses of exotic wildlife below. Experienced guides ensure safety and provide insights into the rainforest's ecosystem, making it an educational adventure for all ages.

Hiking: For those who prefer exploring on foot, Saint Lucia's rainforest trails offer a plethora of hiking opportunities. The Enbas Saut Trail in the Edmund Forest Reserve is a favorite among hikers, leading to a stunning waterfall where you can cool off in natural pools. The trail winds through dense foliage, showcasing endemic flora and fauna, including colorful birds and tropical plants.

Another popular hiking destination is the Gros Piton Nature Trail, a UNESCO World Heritage Site. This challenging but rewarding hike ascends the iconic Gros Piton, offering breathtaking views of the island's southern coast and neighboring peaks. Guides are available to lead hikers and provide historical and ecological insights along the way.

Both zip-lining and hiking in Saint Lucia's rainforests promise unforgettable experiences that combine adventure with the island's natural beauty. Whether you're soaring through the canopy on a zip line or trekking along scenic trails, these activities immerse you in Saint Lucia's pristine landscapes, making it a must-do for outdoor enthusiasts and nature lovers visiting the Caribbean.

Best Beaches (Anse Chastanet, Reduit Beach)

Saint Lucia is renowned for its picturesque beaches, each offering unique charms and opportunities for relaxation and recreation. Here are two of the island's standout beaches that promise unforgettable experiences:

Anse Chastanet

Anse Chastanet
VW7F+W3P, Mamin, St Lucia

Directions

4.7 ★★★★★

View larger map

Jerome Taxi Service

Anse Chastanet
Beach
Scenic beach
for swimming
& snorkeling

Anse Chastanet
4.7 ★ (305)
4-star hotel

Anse Chastanet

Jade Mountain Resort
4.7 ★ (460)
5-star hotel

Scuba St Lucia

Google

Keyboard shortcuts   Map data ©2024   Terms

1. Open the camera app on your phone or tablet.
2. Point the camera at the QR code, making sure it's centered and in focus.
3. Hold the camera steady for a few seconds to allow the code to be detected.
4. Tap the pop-up notification or prompt to open the link or perform the action associated with the QR code.
5. Wait for the action to complete, such as opening a website, downloading an app, or displaying a message.

Anse Chastanet Beach: Nestled between the majestic Piton mountains near Soufrière, Anse Chastanet Beach is a secluded haven for travelers seeking tranquility and natural beauty. The soft, volcanic black sand contrasts with the crystal-clear turquoise waters, creating a stunning backdrop for sunbathing and swimming. Snorkeling enthusiasts can explore vibrant coral reefs just off the shore, teeming with colorful marine life. The beach is part of the Anse Chastanet Resort, which provides amenities like beach loungers, umbrellas, and a beachfront restaurant offering delectable Caribbean cuisine. Visitors can also indulge in spa treatments or enjoy panoramic views of the Pitons from the resort's hillside vantage points.

Reduit Beach: Located in the popular Rodney Bay area, Reduit Beach is celebrated for its expansive stretch of soft, golden sand and calm, shallow waters. This family-friendly beach offers a wide range of activities, from swimming and sunbathing to water sports such as jet skiing and sailing. The nearby Rodney Bay Marina provides opportunities for boat tours and excursions, allowing visitors to explore nearby islands or enjoy sunset cruises along the coast. Numerous beachfront cafes, bars, and shops line the shore, offering refreshments and souvenirs. Reduit Beach's vibrant atmosphere and scenic views make it a favorite destination for both locals and tourists alike, ideal for relaxing days by the sea or lively beachfront gatherings.

Visiting Anse Chastanet and Reduit Beach allows you to experience the diversity of Saint Lucia's coastal beauty, from secluded serenity to vibrant beachfront activity. Whether you seek solitude amidst natural splendor or lively beachside adventures, these beaches offer something special for every traveler, ensuring a memorable and rejuvenating escape in the Caribbean.

Snorkeling and Diving Spots

Saint Lucia, nestled in the heart of the Caribbean, beckons travelers with its pristine waters and vibrant marine life, making it a paradise for snorkelers and divers alike. The island's diverse underwater landscape offers an array of captivating spots to explore, each promising unique encounters with its rich aquatic biodiversity.

Anse Chastanet Reef, near Soufrière, stands out as a favorite among snorkeling and diving enthusiasts. Here, the beach's volcanic black sand meets crystal-clear turquoise waters, where shallow reefs host an abundance of colorful fish and occasional sea turtles. Adventurers can venture deeper to discover intricate caves and dramatic underwater cliffs adorned with thriving coral gardens.

Further along Saint Lucia's southwest coast lies Sugar Beach Reef, also known as the Jalousie Underwater Reserve. This renowned spot entices visitors with its clear, tranquil waters and a mosaic of marine life. Coral gardens provide sanctuary to a kaleidoscope of tropical fish, offering snorkelers and divers alike the chance to witness majestic creatures like reef sharks and barracudas gliding through deeper waters.

For a truly awe-inspiring experience, the Pitons Marine Reserve showcases the island's natural wonders on a

UNESCO World Heritage stage. Spanning the waters between the iconic Piton mountains, this protected area boasts volcanic formations and underwater cliffs draped with vibrant corals. Here, divers and snorkelers can immerse themselves in a world where colorful reef fish dart among swaying sea fans, while sea turtles gracefully navigate the ocean depths.

Navigating these underwater realms requires a blend of respect for the delicate ecosystem and a sense of adventure. Certified guides ensure safety and provide insights into each site's ecological significance, enhancing the experience with expert knowledge. Whether exploring shallow reefs or descending into the depths, every snorkeling and diving excursion in Saint Lucia promises not just a glimpse, but a profound immersion into the island's natural splendor beneath the waves.

Sailing and Boat Tours

Lucia's captivating coastline and tranquil Caribbean waters beckon travelers to explore its natural beauty aboard sailing and boat tours, offering an immersive way to experience the island's charm and adventure.

Embarking on a catamaran cruise is a favorite choice among visitors. These spacious vessels gracefully glide over the azure sea, providing panoramic views of Saint Lucia's lush landscapes and inviting beaches. Many tours include stops at iconic spots like Marigot Bay, celebrated for its serene waters and vibrant marine life. Guests often have the chance to snorkel in crystal-clear waters, discovering colorful fish and coral reefs beneath the surface, adding an exhilarating touch to their journey.

As the day draws to a close, sunset cruises offer a magical experience. Imagine sipping on tropical cocktails while witnessing Saint Lucia's spectacular sunsets casting a golden glow over the towering Piton mountains and tranquil Caribbean waters. Some cruises extend the enchantment with dinner options featuring local flavors, creating unforgettable moments against the backdrop of the island's twilight beauty.

For those seeking a more active adventure, fishing charters provide thrilling opportunities to explore Saint Lucia's deep-sea fishing grounds. Experienced guides lead expeditions in pursuit of prized game fish such as marlin, dorado, and tuna. Whether you're a seasoned angler or new to fishing, these charters offer an exciting chance to reel in your catch amidst the stunning coastal scenery.

Private boat tours cater to personalized experiences, allowing guests to tailor their itinerary to suit their preferences. Discover secluded coves, snorkel in untouched reefs, or visit hidden beaches accessible only by boat. Knowledgeable guides enrich the journey with local insights and stories, offering a deeper connection to Saint Lucia's culture and history.

Throughout these experiences, safety and comfort are paramount, ensuring a seamless and enjoyable adventure on the water. Whether you're exploring with loved ones, friends, or embarking on a romantic getaway, Saint Lucia's sailing and boat tours promise an unforgettable fusion of discovery, relaxation, and the sheer beauty of the Caribbean seascape.

Diamond Falls Botanical Gardens: Diamond Falls Botanical Gardens is a serene oasis nestled in the heart of Soufrière, Saint Lucia. This botanical paradise enchants visitors with its lush greenery, vibrant blooms, and picturesque waterfalls. Established in the late 18th century, the gardens boast a rich history and showcase a diverse collection of tropical plants and flowers, including exotic orchids and colorful heliconias. The highlight of the gardens is the Diamond Waterfall, where mineral-rich waters cascade down a cliffside, creating a stunning backdrop of natural beauty. Visitors can explore winding paths that lead through the gardens, offering glimpses of rare flora and providing a peaceful retreat immersed in Saint Lucia's tropical splendor.

Tet Paul Nature Trail: Tet Paul Nature Trail offers a scenic and educational trek through the lush landscapes near Soufrière, Saint Lucia. This moderate hiking trail provides breathtaking views of the island's iconic Piton mountains and the Caribbean Sea. Along the way, visitors encounter diverse flora and fauna native to the region, including medicinal plants and tropical birds. The trail is renowned for its panoramic viewpoints, where hikers can capture stunning vistas of Saint Lucia's southwestern coast and neighboring islands. Tet Paul Nature Trail offers both a recreational escape and an opportunity to appreciate the natural beauty and cultural heritage of Saint Lucia's countryside.

Anse Mamin Beach: Anse Mamin Beach is a secluded gem tucked away near Soufrière, Saint Lucia, offering a tranquil escape for nature enthusiasts and beachgoers alike. This pristine beach is known for its unspoiled beauty, with soft white sands framed by lush tropical greenery. Surrounded by gently rolling hills and swaying palms, Anse Mamin Beach provides a serene setting for relaxation and exploration. The waters are calm and inviting, perfect for swimming and snorkeling among vibrant coral reefs teeming with marine life. Accessible via a short walk or bike ride from neighboring Anse Chastanet, Anse Mamin Beach promises a peaceful retreat in the midst of Saint Lucia's natural splendor.

Rainforest Adventures Saint Lucia: Rainforest Adventures Saint Lucia offers an exhilarating eco-adventure in the heart of Saint Lucia's lush rainforest. This attraction provides visitors with a chance to explore the island's natural beauty and biodiversity through various activities. One of the highlights is the aerial tram tour, where guests glide through the canopy, enjoying panoramic views of the rainforest and spotting diverse flora and fauna. The adrenaline seekers can opt for ziplining adventures, zooming through the treetops and experiencing the thrill of flying over the forest floor. Guided nature walks provide educational insights into the rainforest's ecology, highlighting medicinal plants and wildlife habitats. Rainforest Adventures Saint Lucia is an ideal destination for nature lovers and adventure enthusiasts seeking an immersive experience in Saint Lucia's rich natural environment.

Soufrière Drive-In Volcano: Soufrière Drive-In Volcano offers a unique geological experience in Saint Lucia, allowing visitors to drive right up to the world's only drive-in volcano. Located near Soufrière town, this dormant volcano's main feature is its bubbling sulfur springs and therapeutic mud baths. Guests can witness the geothermal activity up close, with steam vents emitting sulfuric gases and hot springs bubbling with mineral-rich waters. The area's unique landscape, characterized by volcanic ash and vibrant mineral deposits, provides a fascinating glimpse into the island's volcanic past. Soufrière Drive-In Volcano is not only an educational attraction but also offers visitors a chance to relax and rejuvenate in natural mud baths believed to have therapeutic properties.

Friday Night Street Party: Friday Night Street Party in Gros Islet, Saint Lucia, is a vibrant and lively celebration that brings together locals and tourists alike for an evening of music, dancing, and delicious street food. Held every Friday night, the atmosphere comes alive with Caribbean rhythms, as local bands and DJs fill the air with lively tunes. Visitors can stroll through the bustling streets lined with food stalls offering a variety of local delicacies such as grilled seafood, jerk chicken, and traditional dishes like rice and peas. The party extends late into the night, creating a festive ambiance where everyone can join in the fun, dance under the stars, and immerse themselves in Saint Lucia's rich cultural heritage.

Toraille Waterfall: Toraille Waterfall is a picturesque natural attraction located near Soufrière, Saint Lucia, offering visitors a serene retreat amidst tropical greenery. Cascading from a height of about 50 feet, this majestic waterfall creates a refreshing pool at its base, inviting visitors to cool off in its crystal-clear waters. Surrounded by lush vegetation and tropical flowers, Toraille Waterfall provides a peaceful setting for relaxation and photography. Accessible via a short walk through a verdant garden, the waterfall is a popular stop for tourists exploring the scenic beauty of Saint Lucia's southwest coast.

Gros Islet: Gros Islet is a vibrant village located on the northern tip of Saint Lucia, known for its lively atmosphere, beautiful beaches, and rich cultural heritage. The village is famous for its Friday Night Street Party, where locals and visitors gather to enjoy music, dance, and authentic Caribbean cuisine served by street vendors. Gros Islet also boasts stunning beaches like Reduit Beach, popular for its soft sands and clear waters ideal for swimming and water sports. Visitors can explore the local markets, dine at seaside restaurants, and experience the warm hospitality of the community. Gros Islet offers a blend of relaxation, cultural immersion, and nightlife, making it a must-visit destination in Saint Lucia.

Morne Coubaril Historical Adventure Park: Morne Coubaril Historical Adventure Park offers a fascinating blend of history, adventure, and natural beauty in Saint Lucia. Located near Soufrière, this park allows visitors to step back in time and experience the island's agricultural history firsthand. The park features a working plantation where traditional crops like cocoa and coffee are grown, showcasing Saint Lucia's rich agricultural heritage. Visitors can take guided tours to learn about the plantation's history, see historic artifacts, and witness demonstrations of traditional farming techniques. Additionally, Morne Coubaril Historical Adventure Park offers thrilling activities such as zip-lining through the rainforest canopy and horseback riding with panoramic views of the Pitons and Caribbean Sea. It's a perfect destination for those seeking both cultural insights and outdoor adventure in Saint Lucia.

Pointe Seraphine Cruise Port: Pointe Seraphine Cruise Port is a prominent cruise terminal located in Castries, Saint Lucia, catering to international cruise ships visiting the island. Situated on the northwest coast near the capital city, Pointe Seraphine is a gateway for tourists to explore Saint Lucia's attractions, shopping, and cultural offerings. The port features duty-free shopping boutiques offering a variety of goods such as jewelry, local crafts, souvenirs, and luxury items. Visitors can also find restaurants, cafes, and bars within the port area, providing a convenient spot to relax and enjoy Caribbean cuisine and beverages. With its scenic views of the harbor and convenient access to Castries' attractions, Pointe Seraphine Cruise Port serves as a welcoming introduction to the beauty and culture of Saint Lucia for cruise passengers.

CHAPTER 9:
FOOD, DINING,
AND SHOPPING

S aint Lucian cuisine is a delightful fusion of African, Caribbean, and French influences, showcasing fresh ingredients and bold flavor Here are some must-try dishes and local favorites:

Green Fig and Saltfish: A traditional breakfast dish made with green bananas (referred to locally as "green fig") boiled and served with salted codfish cooked with onions, tomatoes, and spices.

Callaloo Soup: A hearty soup made from callaloo leaves (similar to spinach), okra, coconut milk, and often flavored with meat or seafood. It's a comforting and nutritious choice.

Roti: Influenced by Indian cuisine, roti in Saint Lucia typically consists of a thin flatbread filled with curried chicken, beef, or vegetables, served with a side of mango chutney.

Accra: Fried fritters made from salted codfish, flour, and various herbs and spices. They're crispy on the outside and soft on the inside, often served as a snack or appetizer.

Bouyon: A hearty stew featuring meat (typically chicken or pork), root vegetables like dasheen (taro), yams, and plantains, simmered in a flavorful broth with herbs and spices.

Piton Beer: The local beer named after the iconic Piton mountains. It's a refreshing choice to accompany meals or enjoy on its own.

Chocolate: Saint Lucia is known for its cocoa production, and chocolate lovers can indulge in locally made chocolate bars, truffles, and hot cocoa drinks.

Grilled Fish: With its coastal location, fresh fish such as mahi-mahi or kingfish is often marinated and grilled to perfection, served with sides like rice and beans or fried plantains.

Exploring Saint Lucian cuisine offers a taste of the island's rich cultural heritage and the bounty of its tropical surroundings. Each dish reflects the warmth and flavors of the Caribbean, making dining an essential part of the Saint Lucian experience.

Top Restaurants and Dining Experiences

Saint Lucia offers a diverse culinary scene with a range of dining options that cater to every taste and preference. Here are some top restaurants and dining experiences to explore on the island:

Boucan by Hotel Chocolat: Located in Soufrière, this restaurant offers a unique dining experience focused on cacao-inspired cuisine. Dishes feature locally sourced ingredients paired with chocolate-infused flavors, complemented by stunning views of the Pitons.

The Coal Pot: Situated in Castries, The Coal Pot is renowned for its seafood dishes and Creole-inspired cuisine. It's a waterfront restaurant offering a cozy atmosphere and delicious meals prepared with fresh, local ingredients.

Dasheene at Ladera Resort: Known for its breathtaking views of the Caribbean Sea and Pitons, Dasheene serves up Caribbean flavors with a gourmet twist. The restaurant emphasizes farm-to-table dining, featuring dishes that highlight Saint Lucian spices and produce.

Orlando's Restaurant and Bar: Located in Soufrière, Orlando's is a local favorite known for its authentic Saint Lucian dishes. It offers a casual dining experience with a focus on seafood, grilled meats, and traditional Creole cuisine.

Cap Maison: Situated in Cap Estate, this restaurant combines French Caribbean influences with Mediterranean flavors. Cap Maison offers fine dining in an elegant setting, with a renowned wine cellar and panoramic views of the ocean.

The Cliff at Cap: Also located in Cap Estate, The Cliff at Cap offers a romantic setting perched above the sea. It features a blend of French and Caribbean cuisines, accompanied by live music and stunning sunset views.

Jambe de Bois: This casual beachfront restaurant on Pigeon Island National Park offers a laid-back atmosphere and

Caribbean comfort food. It's a great spot to enjoy seafood, burgers, and cocktails while soaking in the island vibe.

Spice of India: For those craving international flavors, Spice of India in Rodney Bay serves authentic Indian cuisine with a view of the marina. It's a popular choice for its flavorful curries, tandoori dishes, and vegetarian options.

Fire Grill Steakhouse & Lounge Bar: Located in Rodney Bay, Fire Grill is known for its sizzling steaks, burgers, and seafood. It offers a relaxed atmosphere with live music and a diverse menu that caters to meat lovers and vegetarians alike.

Ti Kaye Resort & Spa: This resort's oceanfront restaurant offers a romantic dining experience with panoramic views and a menu that focuses on fresh seafood and Creole dishes, paired with an extensive wine list.

These dining establishments showcase the diversity and richness of Saint Lucian cuisine, offering memorable experiences that blend local flavors with international influences in beautiful settings across the island.

Street Food and Markets

In Saint Lucia, exploring street food and local markets offers a vibrant culinary adventure filled with flavors and cultural insights. Here are some highlights of street food and markets you can enjoy:

Castries Market: Located in the capital city, Castries, this bustling market is a hub of activity where you can find fresh produce, spices, crafts, and street food. Try local favorites like grilled fish, roti, and accra (saltfish fritters) from various vendors.

Anse La Raye Fish Fry: Every Friday evening, the fishing village of Anse La Raye comes alive with its weekly fish fry. Sample freshly caught seafood like grilled lobster, fish, and conch, along with sides like rice and peas, johnny cakes, and plantains.

Gros Islet Street Party: Held every Friday night in Gros Islet, this street party is a lively affair featuring music, dancing, and street food. Try barbecue specialties, seafood dishes, and local snacks while enjoying the festive atmosphere.

Dennery Fish Fiesta: In Dennery, a town known for its fishing community, the Fish Fiesta offers a chance to taste a variety of seafood dishes prepared by local vendors. It's a great opportunity to savor fresh catches cooked in traditional Saint Lucian styles.

Rodney Bay Village: Rodney Bay offers a mix of restaurants, bars, and food stalls where you can sample Caribbean street food. Look for vendors selling grilled meats, creole dishes, and refreshing beverages like coconut water or fresh fruit juices.

Local Snacks: Throughout the island, you'll find vendors selling traditional snacks such as bakes (fried dough), saltfish cakes, and pastries filled with local fruits like guava or banana.

Marigot Bay Market: Explore this picturesque bay and visit the local market where vendors sell fresh fruits, vegetables, and snacks. It's a quieter spot compared to larger markets but offers a glimpse into daily life on the island.

Saint Lucia's street food and markets not only satisfy culinary cravings but also provide a glimpse into the island's vibrant culture and community spirit. Whether you're exploring a bustling market or enjoying a casual street-side meal, you'll find warmth, flavor, and a true taste of Saint Lucia.

Souvenirs and Local Crafts

When visiting Saint Lucia, exploring local crafts and souvenirs offers a wonderful way to take home a piece of the island's rich culture and craftsmanship. Here are some popular souvenirs and local crafts to look out for:

Handmade Pottery: Saint Lucia is known for its pottery, often crafted with vibrant colors and intricate designs. Look for bowls, vases, and decorative items that reflect the island's natural beauty and artistic flair.

Batik Clothing: Batik fabric is a traditional craft in Saint Lucia, featuring unique patterns and colors. You can find batik clothing such as dresses, shirts, and sarongs that showcase the island's craftsmanship and style.

Local Artwork: Explore galleries and local markets for paintings, sculptures, and mixed-media artwork created by Saint Lucian artists. Themes often include tropical landscapes, marine life, and cultural scenes.

Jewelry: Handmade jewelry using local materials like shells, coral, and semi-precious stones is popular in Saint Lucia. Look for earrings, necklaces, and bracelets that highlight the island's natural beauty and craftsmanship.

Coconut Products: From coconut shell carvings to coconut oil and beauty products, coconut-based crafts and products are widely available in Saint Lucia. These items showcase the island's sustainable practices and cultural traditions.

Spices and Seasonings: Take home a taste of Saint Lucia with locally produced spices and seasonings. Look for blends like Creole seasoning, cocoa tea mix, and hot sauces made with scotch bonnet peppers.

Rum and Cocoa Products: Saint Lucia is renowned for its rum and cocoa production. Purchase locally made rum, chocolate bars, and cocoa-based products such as cocoa tea or cocoa nibs to enjoy a taste of the island's flavors.

Handwoven Baskets and Crafts: Explore markets for handwoven baskets, mats, and other crafts made from natural fibers like straw and bamboo. These items often feature traditional designs and techniques passed down through generations.

Caribelle Batik: Visit Caribelle Batik at the historic Romney Manor in St. Kitts to shop for batik clothing, accessories, and home décor items crafted using traditional methods.

Musical Instruments: Look for handmade drums, steel pans, and other musical instruments that reflect Saint Lucia's vibrant music scene and cultural heritage.

Exploring souvenirs and local crafts in Saint Lucia not only supports local artisans but also provides unique mementos that capture the essence of the island's beauty, culture, and creativity. Whether you're looking for artwork, clothing, or culinary delights, Saint Lucia offers a treasure trove of handmade treasures to cherish.

Chapter 10: Sample Itineraries and Bonus Section

E mbark on a journey through Saint Lucia with this comprehensive 10-day itinerary. Designed to capture the island's vibrant culture stunning, landscapes, and unforgettable expe riences, this plan will ensure that you make the most of your visit.

Day 1: Arrival and Castries Exploration

Morning: Arrive at Hewanorra International Airport and transfer to your hotel in Castries.

Afternoon: Explore Castries Market for local crafts, spices, and fresh produce.

Evening: Enjoy a welcome dinner at a local restaurant, savoring traditional Saint Lucian cuisine.

Day 2: Historical and Cultural Highlights

Morning: Visit the Cathedral of the Immaculate Conception and Derek Walcott Square.

Afternoon: Tour the Pointe Seraphine duty-free shopping complex.

Evening: Stroll through Rodney Bay Village, exploring boutiques and dining options.

Day 3: Natural Wonders and Adventure

Morning: Head to the Diamond Falls Botanical Gardens to marvel at the vibrant flora and the stunning waterfall.

Afternoon: Enjoy a guided tour of the Soufrière Drive-In Volcano, followed by a relaxing soak in the nearby mud baths.

Evening: Dinner in Soufrière, with a view of the iconic Pitons.

Day 4: Rainforest and Nature Trails

Morning: Take the Tet Paul Nature Trail for breathtaking views and a closer look at the island's flora and fauna.

Afternoon: Experience the thrill of zip-lining with Rainforest Adventures Saint Lucia.

Evening: Return to your hotel and relax after an adventurous day.

Day 5: Beach and Water Activities

Morning: Spend the morning at Anse Chastanet Beach, enjoying snorkeling and sunbathing.

Afternoon: Continue your beach day at Anse Mamin Beach, known for its tranquility and beauty.

Evening: Beachfront dinner with fresh seafood and tropical cocktails.

Day 6: Maritime Adventures

Morning: Set sail on a boat tour exploring the stunning coastline and secluded bays of Saint Lucia.

Afternoon: Engage in snorkeling or diving at one of the island's top spots.

Evening: Return to your hotel and enjoy a leisurely evening.

Day 7: Local Culture and Festivities

Morning: Visit the Marigot Bay for its serene beauty and charming shops.

Afternoon: Tour the Morne Coubaril Historical Adventure Park, learning about Saint Lucia's colonial history and plantation life.

Evening: Join the Gros Islet Friday Night Street Party for local music, dance, and street food.

Day 8: Exploring Soufrière and Surroundings

Morning: Discover the hidden gem of Toraille Waterfall and take a refreshing dip.

Afternoon: Visit the Grand Eden Estate for a tour of their lush gardens and local farming practices.

Evening: Enjoy a quiet evening in Soufrière, dining at a local eatery.

Day 9: Leisure and Relaxation

Morning: Relax at your hotel or explore nearby attractions at your own pace.

Afternoon: Spend some time shopping for souvenirs and local crafts.

Evening: Indulge in a romantic dinner at one of Saint Lucia's luxury resorts.

Day 10: Farewell Saint Lucia

Morning: Take one last walk along the beach or a final dip in the ocean.

Afternoon: Prepare for your departure, ensuring all travel documents are in order.

Evening: Depart from Hewanorra International Airport with unforgettable memories of your Saint Lucia adventure.

This 10-day itinerary offers a balanced mix of adventure, relaxation, cultural immersion, and culinary delights, making your stay in Saint Lucia truly memorable.

Smartphone Photography Tips for Beautiful Crystal Photos

Smartphone photography has revolutionized the way we capture and share moments, allowing everyone to become a photographer with just a few taps. Here are some tips to help you take stunning, crystal-clear photos with your smartphone:

1. Clean Your Lens: Before you start shooting, make sure your smartphone's lens is clean. Dust, fingerprints, and smudges can significantly affect the quality of your photos. Use a soft, microfiber cloth to gently wipe the lens.

2. Use Natural Light: Lighting is crucial in photography. Natural light usually provides the best results, so try to shoot in well-lit environments. Early morning or late afternoon light, known as the "golden hour," can give your photos a warm, soft glow.

3. Steady Your Shot: Keep your smartphone steady to avoid blurry photos. Use both hands to hold your phone or prop it against a stable surface. Alternatively, consider using a small tripod or a stabilizer for even better stability.

4. Focus and Exposure: Tap on the screen to focus on your subject. This will also adjust the exposure automatically. If your photo looks too dark or too bright, you can manually adjust the exposure by sliding your finger up or down on the screen.

5. Use the Rule of Thirds: Activate the gridlines on your camera settings to help compose your shots using the rule of thirds. Place your subject along the lines or at the intersections to create a balanced and visually appealing photo.

6. Explore Different Angles: Don't just settle for eye-level shots. Experiment with different angles and perspectives to add variety and interest to your photos. Try shooting from above, below, or from the side to see how it changes the composition.

7. Utilize HDR Mode: High Dynamic Range (HDR) mode helps balance the light and dark areas in your photo, capturing more detail in both the shadows and highlights. Use HDR mode in high-contrast scenes for a more balanced exposure.

8. Edit Your Photos: Post-processing can enhance your photos and correct any imperfections. Use photo editing apps like Snapseed, VSCO, or Lightroom to adjust brightness, contrast, saturation, and sharpness. Apply filters sparingly to maintain a natural look.

9. Avoid Digital Zoom: Digital zoom can degrade the quality of your photos by making them grainy or pixelated. Instead of zooming in, move closer to your subject or crop the photo afterward to maintain clarity.

10. Use Portrait Mode: If your smartphone has a portrait mode, use it to create a shallow depth of field effect, which blurs the background and makes your subject stand out. This is great for portrait shots and close-up photography.

11. Pay Attention to Backgrounds: A cluttered or distracting background can take away from your main subject. Look for clean, simple backgrounds or use the camera's focus feature to blur the background and make your subject pop.

12. Keep Practicing: The more you practice, the better you'll become at smartphone photography. Experiment with different settings, compositions, and lighting conditions to discover what works best for you.

With these tips, you'll be well on your way to capturing beautiful, crystal-clear photos with your smartphone, making your memories look professional and Instagram-worthy.

```
Z  A  D  T  F  B  X  P  D  W  R  E  E  E  R
A  H  X  S  L  E  C  I  L  A  O  R  X  T  O
W  T  D  U  X  A  S  U  I  A  T  U  P  A  V
E  M  T  M  T  C  S  N  U  R  N  T  L  G  A
V  X  H  R  O  H  F  P  O  Q  E  N  O  I  S
G  E  P  V  A  O  R  P  I  E  R  E  R  V  I
B  N  E  E  R  C  S  I  S  T  O  V  E  A  E
E  R  I  E  R  N  T  I  L  P  L  D  H  N  G
A  N  S  N  A  I  D  I  M  L  L  A  C  O  L
U  T  I  R  N  A  E  D  O  E  I  D  V  Z  U
T  L  T  S  R  U  Q  N  G  N  G  N  J  H  D
Y  A  B  A  I  Q  T  V  C  N  S  M  G  Z  N
Z  H  P  L  M  U  M  S  R  E  D  I  S  N  I
R  P  E  R  F  E  C  T  E  R  U  T  L  U  C
A  C  C  O  M  M  O  D  A  T  I  O  N  S  Q
```

Find These Words in the Puzzle

Beach	Discover	Thrilling
Rainforest	Local	Indulge
Culture	Gem	Insider
Cuisine	Navigate	Tips
Adventure	Paradise	Must-see
Transport	Experience	Perfect
Accommodations	Beauty	Visitors
Attractions	Stunning	Seasoned
Explore	Savor	Travelers
Unforgetable	Plan	Immersive

```
E  L  B  A  Y  U  J  Z  I  P  F  T  S  B  X
R  F  A  O  Q  O  G  E  M  S  P  L  T  O  A
U  W  W  I  U  V  D  C  Y  I  L  V  E  A  L
T  A  G  R  T  L  Q  S  Z  U  E  A  S  T  E
A  T  N  N  G  N  I  L  E  K  R  O  N  S  R
N  E  M  K  I  F  E  V  L  W  O  T  U  D  F
Y  R  V  A  G  L  A  S  X  D  L  O  S  J  S
C  F  H  A  R  N  I  U  S  R  P  O  X  W  G
R  A  A  K  C  K  I  A  N  E  X  V  E  N  N
A  L  R  K  X  A  E  N  S  A  E  I  E  D  I
F  L  B  B  Z  E  T  T  I  M  V  D  I  L  K
T  S  O  P  N  K  P  I  S  D  D  V  A  N  I
S  L  R  E  D  I  U  G  O  I  I  R  T  K  H
L  I  N  I  N  G  M  X  H  N  O  K  Y  P  G
G  N  I  P  P  O  H  S  G  C  R  E  E  F  S
```

Find These Words in the Puzzle

Bay	Gems	Reefs
Boats	Guide	Relax
Coral	Harbor	Sailing
Crafts	Hidden	Shopping
Dining	Hiking	Snorkeling
Diving	Islands	Sunsets
Dream	Journey	Vacation
Essential	lining	Views
Explore	Markets	Waterfalls
Fauna	Nature	Zip

Seeking Your Insight, Share with Us

Dear Reader,

We hope you enjoyed exploring our St. Lucia travel guide and found it helpful in planning your journey. Your experience and opinions are invaluable to us, and we are committed to continually improving our guides to better serve you and future travelers.

We kindly invite you to share your thoughts and feedback through a review on the platform where you found this guide. What aspects of the guide did you find most useful? Were there any sections that particularly resonated with you or any areas where you felt we could enhance your experience? Your detailed insights help us create even more comprehensive and engaging guides.

Your review not only assists us in refining our content but also aids fellow travelers in making informed decisions. Your voice matters, and we genuinely appreciate the time you take to share your perspectives.

Thank you for your support and contribution.

Warm regards,

[James Atlas Venture]

Made in the USA
Monee, IL
19 September 2024

66134690R00056